T0107993

Solidarity or Egoism

Voters in Scandinavia · 1

THE ROCKWOOL FOUNDATION RESEARCH UNIT

Douglas Hibbs

Solidarity or Egoism?

The Economics of Sociotropic and Egocentric
Influences on Political Behavior:
Denmark in International and Theoretical
Perspective

AARHUS UNIVERSITY PRESS

Copyright: Aarhus University Press, 1993
Word-processed by the author
Cover design by Poul Nørbo
Printed in England by the Alden Press, Oxford
Produced on permanent paper conforming to ANSI standard Z39-48.1984
ISBN 87 7288 452 5

AARHUS UNIVERSITY PRESS
Building 170
Aarhus University
DK-8000 Aarhus C, Denmark
Fax + 45 86 19 84 33

Contents

SOLIDARITY OR EGOISM

List of Tables

Preface

A recurring topic in Danish public debate is the relationship between the electorate and the politicians. Many political observers have pointed to an increasing distrust of politicians among the electorate, and this view is confirmed by several present and past MPs. At the same time the sense of a confidence crisis is nourished by spectacular headlines in the daily press featuring yet another political scandal almost daily.

Lately, the trust and confidence issue seems to have acquired additional accent as a consequence of the referendums concerning Danish ratification of the Maastricht Treaty. The first, which took place in June 1992, resulted in a narrow no-vote, despite a yes-vote recommendation by the Parliamentary Parties and a strong majority of the 179 MPs, the majority of the nation's professional and industrial associations, and the labor unions. And even though the second referendum in May 1993, undertaken after concessions were made to Denmark in the Edinburgh agreements, produced a 57 percent yes-vote, a large fraction of the electorate nonetheless voted against the recommendations of the established political parties.

On the basis of these and other signs of a confidence crisis, the Rockwool Foundation Research Unit at Danmarks Statistik (the Danish Central Bureau of Statistics), which during the last five years has specialized in analyses of important questions facing Danish society, decided that the issue was significant enough to warrant a new research effort focused on the relationship between the Danish electorate and their parliamentary representatives and, more generally, the Danish electorate's perception of their political system.

The research project was launched in 1989, with intensive collection of data carried out in 1990 and 1991. The results of the research appeared subsequently in April 1992 in two publications: *Vi og vore politikere (We and Our Politicians)* and *Kan vi stole på politikerne? (Can Politicians be Trusted?)*. In *Vi og vore politikere* the results were presented in greater detail, whereas *Kan vi stole på politikerne?*, written by the undersigned, contained a more accessible summary of the research.

During the work in the Rockwool Foundation Research Unit on the electorate's confidence and trust in politicians and the political system, the researchers became aware of a controversy concerning the interpretation of recent Danish research about a related subject - namely the degree to which Danish voters are motivated by conceptions of the public interest as opposed to calculations of private economic interest (often designated "pocketbook" voting). Some researchers reached the conclusions that the political opinions and behavior of Danes exhibited considerably greater egoism than had been reported in similar research on other countries. Other researchers concluded that the Danish electorate conformed more or less to the patterns typical elsewhere in Scandinavia.

After termination of the main project on political trust and confidence, the Rockwool Foundation Research Unit therefore asked one of the leading experts in this field, Dr. Douglas Hibbs - earlier Professor at MIT and Harvard University, now Senior Research Fellow at the FIEF Institute in Stockholm - to undertake a critical evaluation of the results available for Denmark and to a lessor degree the rest of Scandinavia, and the outcome of this effort is presented herein.

Finally, it should be noted that this study, as earlier projects in the Rockwool Foundation Research Unit, has been carried out in complete scientific independence. The research would, however, have been impossible to carry out without the interest and support of the Rockwool Foundation and the cooperation of Director Bent Løber and the Chairman of the Board, Group President and Chief Executive Tom Kähler.

Gunnar Viby Mogensen, Copenhagen, August 1993

In the last analysis the people will judge the revolution by this fact alone — does it take more or less money? Are they better off? Do they have more work? And is that work better paid?
            Mirabeau (1791)

The passion for equality seeps into every corner of the human heart, expands and fills the whole. It is no use telling them that by this blind surrender to an exclusive passion they are compromising their dearest interests; they are deaf.
            Tocqueville (1835)

I.
The Intellectual Origins of the Egocentric-Sociotropic Debate

The strong historical presumption of economic theory, from the time of Adam Smith and before, is that individual economic behavior is to a rather good first approximation governed wholly by attempts to maximize self-interest, from which, as every entry-level student of economics is instructed, much common benefit may flow. Formal and quantitative analyses of economic influences on political behavior, originating in large part with Kramer's path-breaking 1971 study of US congressional voting behavior, and the focus of many hundreds of studies since,[1] were either implicitly or explicitly based on this traditional *homo economicus* assumption: Empirically well established relations between macroeconomic conditions and political opinions and behavior were aggregate reflections of rational, micro-level self-interested behavior. As Downs put it "each citizen casts his vote for the party he believes will provide him with more benefits than any other." (Downs, 1957, p. 36)

In the economics and political behavior literature the self-interest presumption became known as "pocketbook" voting — voters rewarded parties that advanced their own economic interests and punished those that threatened them. The pocketbook or "egocentric" view (as I shall frequently refer to it ahead) was the prevailing explanation, at least implicitly, of aggregate connections between economics and politics until Kinder and Kiewet's work appeared in the late 1970s and early 1980s. (Kinder and Kiewet, 1979, 1981; Kiewet, 1983; Kinder et al. 1989) Directly confronting the pocketbook hypothesis with micro, survey data on US voting intentions, Kinder and Kiewet made what many regarded as a startling discovery: personal economic experiences appeared to exhibit much weaker

---

1. See the reviews of Paldam (1981) and Nannestad and Paldam (1993b).

connections to electoral behavior[2] than voters' evaluations of national economic conditions and their assessments of the government's performance and competence in dealing with national problems.

Kinder and Kiewet labeled the phenomenon — and the label has stuck — "sociotropic" voting:[3]

The sociotropic voter rewards incumbents for good performance and punishes them for bad[4] ... The sociotropic voter asks political leaders not 'What have you done for *me* lately?' but rather 'What have you done for the *country* lately?' and 'What are you likely to do for the *country* in the future?' Purely sociotropic citizens vote according to the country's pocketbook, not their own. (Kinder and Kiewet, 1981, pp. 156, 132)

I excerpt the core results of Kinder and Kiewet's empirical analysis of survey.data on U.S. Presidential voting in 1972 and 1976 in Table 1. Among the personal or household (egocentric) economic variables, only household unemployment experience exhibited a significant connection to reported Presidential voting in Kinder and Kiewet's regression experiments. And by comparison to the magnitude of effects associated with the public's ratings of the Government's Economic Performance, or to more general perceptions of the Competence of the Democratic and Republican parties in managing national economic problems (inflation and unemployment), egocentric orientations appeared to exert almost negligible influence on American political behavior.

Notice, in particular, the dominant influence of the Party Competence variable, which unfortunately was not available in the 1972 national election study survey that Kinder and Kiewet analyzed. The paramount importance

---

2. Initially, Kinder and Kiewet put the result quite categorically—"Under ordinary circumstances, voters evidently do not make connections between their own personal economic experiences ... and their political attitudes and preferences." (Kinder and Kiewet, 1979, p.522)—but later backed off from this strong view.
3. Although, in more general application, the term apparently was coined by Meehl (1977).
4. An idea, which put in just this form, was first systematically pursued by V.O. Key (1966) and is known as "retrospective" voting. See Fiorina (1978, 1981).

Table 1

Egocentric and Sociotropic Influences on Voting in American Presidential Elections

Egocentric	1972	1976
Household Financial Situation	NS	NS
Household Unemployment	0.07	0.05
Personal Economic Problems	NS	NS
Sociotropic		
National Business Conditions	NS	0.06
National unemployment, Inflation Problems	NS	-0.1
Government Economic Performance	0.27	0.11
Party Economic Competence	NA	0.4

Sources: Kinder and Kiewet, 1981, table 4.
Note: NA = not applicable; NS = not statistically significant.

of assessments of the parties' economic management Competence for American's voting choices is a matter I shall return to later in chapter II, when evaluating the internal consistency of claims made in recent research on Danish political behavior about the dominant role of egocentric motivation.

Kinder and Kiewet were careful to differentiate their conception of sociotropically motivated political behavior from pure altruism, a distinction that unfortunately has been lost in most subsequent discussions. Even the most self-interested of voters may view robust national economic conditions as a public good that confers many private benefits, including enhanced prospects of future private economic mobility, private security, and the well-being (utility) accruing even to the very affluent from living in a society without signs of widespread distress among fellow citizens that typically accompany a moribund macro economy.

Having said this, however, it must be recognized that broadening the conception of egocentric motivation to allow concern about the circumstances of others, makes it almost impossible to reject the egocentric, pocketbook theory of economic voting in data...[5] In other words, egocentric motivation conceived as generously endowed 'enlightened' self-interest cannot be readily distinguished from simple sociotropic behavior.

The first replications and refinements of Kinder and Kiewet's original work were done mainly by other American researchers, and on the whole the results were supportive of the sociotropic thesis. Michael Lewis-Beck's (1988) comparative investigation, based on special questions that he arranged to have added to the regular 1983 and 1984 Eurobarometer Surveys, is probably the most ambitious study. Lewis-Beck reports literally hundreds of regressions and correlations designed to evaluate a wide range of issues in the economics and voting field. Table 2 shows results excerpted from a representative set of his regressions for the five countries analyzed.

Three conclusions may be drawn from Lewis-Beck's comparative regression evidence. First, as in Kinder and Kiewet's germinal studies, sociotropic variables appeared to have much greater impact on European parliamentary voting behavior than egocentric variables. Second, among both classes of variables, questions that explicitly prompted the survey respondents to assess the effect of *Government* on the national economy or their personal economy, generally exerted greater influence than assessments of national or personal economic conditions made without the Government responsibility filter. And, third, the electorate's expectations of the future effect of Government policy on the macroeconomy exhibited as much or more influence on contemporaneous voting behavior as retrospective judgments did. The implications of these conclusions, particularly the first and second, will figure prominently in the sections to follow, which feature recent results obtained for Denmark.

Although Lewis-Beck's study is the most comprehensive investigation of egocentric and sociotropic motivation of voting behavior, the relevant literature is now very large. Lewin (1991, chapter 2), writing with unusual clarity and grace, reviews the most influential work, and concludes that

---

5. In this respect, generous conceptions of enlightened self-interest resemble the economists' hypothesis of utility maximization; an idea which can never be rejected in data so long as it accommodates, by definition, whatever behavior is observed.

Table 2

Egocentric and Sociotropic Influences on Voting in European Parliamentary Elections

1984 Surveys in	UK	France	FRG	Italy	Spain
Personal Finances	NS	NS	NS	NS	NS
National Economy	0.06	0.11	0.04	0.07	0.08
Government on Self	0.07	NS	NS	NS	0.08
Government on National Economy	0.14	NS	0.16	0.07	NS
Future Government Policies on					
National Economy	0.19	0.21	0.18	0.07	0.14
Anger About Government					
Economic Management	0.08	0.08	0.09	0.05	0.07

Sources: Lewis-Beck (1988), table 4.1.
Notes: NS = not statistically significant.

---

homo politicus is quite decisively a sociotropic rather than egocentric creature. (If both he and the classical economists are right, then homo-economicus-politicus must be a schizophrenic.) However, in my view Lewin underweights enormously the importance of Kramer's devastating critique of research based on cross-section data, which comprises nearly all the literature he reviewed. Later on in this monograph I take up this point at some length.

The first systematic evaluation test for Denmark of the importance of sociotropic and egocentric motivation appeared only recently in the works of Jørgen Goul Andersen (1991a, 1992b), Peter Nannestad and Martin Paldam (1991, 1992, and 1993a in progress) and Søren Winter and Poul Erik Mouritzen (1992). Nannestad and Paldam's work is more self-consciously tailored to the international debate and applies higher powered statistical methods than the other studies, and for these reasons is taken as the reference point for much of this monograph.

The remainder of this monograph is organized as follows. Chapter II reviews briefly recent research on Denmark, giving special attention, as noted, to the work of Peter Nannestad and Martin Paldam. Chapter III gives a brief exposition of the pure theory of political choice and develops its implications for assessing the magnitudes of sociotropic and egocentric motivation, and the stability of Danish bloc voting. Chapters IV to VIII derive some standard results from the econometrics of measurement specification error and applies the lessons indicated to conclusions drawn by Nannestad and Paldam about egocentric and sociotropic inspired political behavior in Denmark. Chapter IX describes the evolution of research methods and results in the United States on egocentric and sociotropic voting, which have obvious implications for the interpretation of existing research and the likely orientation of future research on Denmark and other countries. Chapter 10 summarizes and concludes.

on self-interest. I would
es and more spending,
ctor efficiency, 2 or as
many of us to "free-
orical), or simply as
all they are elected,
ims, rather than as
se.
o papers on the
Danish political
ce" of Danish
The first paper
assessment of
n over 1983-
nt's "ability
991).
d Paldam
e in your
eel trust
fronting
uld be
n and
92c),
nent
the
2,

.s the least problemati
.ocuses directly on the
a variable which perhaps is
.o reveal the dimensions of
.itical life. Moreover, the May
pirical base of the investigation
On the other hand, Winter and
.om just one Danish municipality
y bounded in space as well as time.[1]
their data as yielding evidence of both
.he distribution of expenditure preferences.
.f their sample of 3,000 respondents thought
.gh, expenditures on the core welfare state
care of the elderly, education and public
.orted by solid majorities of those expressing
y marginal activities (in terms of the scale of claims
.ike museums and library lending of records seemed
difficulty with the electorate. Fiscal policy preferences
therefore not satisfy ideas about what Renaissance man
.ald be willing to finance out of the public purse, but the
welfare state commitments appear to enjoy broad popular

and Mouritzen also found, however, that support for higher
, or lower user fees was generally greater among program users
.mers) than non-users, which along with the majority preference for
.r tax rates is taken to be evidence of egocentric behavior. The user/non-

---

1. An earlier paper by Mouritzen (1987) analyzed the correlates of popular demand for government expenditure in a national Danish opinion poll, but the independent variables of this study do not well distinguish personal from collective interest.

ndoubtedly does reveal preference based
ed to interpret the preference for lower ta
r, as an implicit demand for greater public s
ction of the seemingly irresistible inclination o
 when given the opportunity (in this case the rhe
appeal to politicians to do the job, for which after
 sorting out conflicting and, at times, irreconcilable cl
vidence of fiscal illusion and egocentric sentiment *per*

Nannestad and Paldam have thus far completed tw
importance of sociotropic and egocentric motivation for
attitudes and behavior. (Nannestad and Paldam, 1991, 1992
(Nannestad and Paldam, 1991) deals with the "Competer
(Bourgeois) governments, as measured by (i) the public's
"how well or badly" the governments' "manage" (surveys take
1988), and (ii) the public's "trust or distrust" of the governme
to solve the tasks confronting it" (surveys taken during 1988-1

The full questions (translated from Danish) in Nannestad a
(1991) are: (i) "How well does the present government manag
opinion? ... Very Badly, Badly, Fairly or Well." And (ii) "Do you
or distrust of the present government's ability to solve the tasks con
it? ... Great Distrust, Distrust, Neither, Trust or Great Trust".[3] It sh
emphasized, as the recent collaborative research of Hans Jørgen Niels
Jørgen Goul Andersen reminds us (Nielsen, 1992, Goul Andersen, 19
that these questions pertain to the Danish public's views of the manage
Competence of *particular* Danish Governments, and not to trust of
political system, governments, or politicians *in general*. As Nielsen (19
p. 38) put it:

The most basic criticism of Danish election studies is almost too simple to be true.
We have studied political distrust for more than twenty years, but have never asked

---

2. Gunnar Viby Mogensen of the Rockwool Foundation Research Unit informs
   me in private communication that unpublished data from a large Danish
   survey implies that around one-third of the respondents prefering lower taxes
   conceived of their attitude as a demand for greater public sector efficiency.
3. In Nannestad and Paldam, 1992, appendix, the second question is translated
   "Do you have trust or distrust in the ability of the present government to solve
   the problems that need to be solved?"

SOLIDARITY OR EGOISM

voters whether they trust politicians or not. Instead we have inquired whether they agreed or disagreed with much more specific questions.

Regressions in Nannestad and Paldam's 1992 paper which include the government Competence variable use the 1988-1991 question and exploit the full range of responses, which are coded +1 ("Great Distrust") to +5 ("Great Trust"). Throughout the Nannestad and Paldam 1991 paper, however, the "Very Badly" and "Badly" responses on the first question, and "Great Distrust" and "Trust" responses from the second, were summed to form binary (and aggregate percentage) indicators of government Competence. This is unfortunate, as it needlessly collapses pretty good four-point-scale and five-point-scale measures of what is of course a continuous dimension (the electorate's underlying assessment of the government's problem solving and management capacity) to simple binary variates. Yet at the same time, in the 1991 paper Nannestad and Paldam implicitly attempt to undo the damage by using dichotomous probit analysis, which is designed to map a binary variate back to a continuous evaluation index.[4] The upshot is unnecessary and potentially great loss of estimation efficiency.[5]

One line of analysis in Nannestad and Paldam's 1991 paper aggregates the binary re-codings of the 1983-88 "manage" question and the 1988-91 "ability" question and strings them together over time to form a 1983-91 aggregate time series of percentage "Competency" ratings. The relation of the aggregate Competency ratings to a number of macroeconomic variables (changes of the inflation or real wage growth rate, changes of the unemployment rate and changes of the balance of payments surplus/deficit) is then investigated via aggregate time series regression.

Figure 1 shows the aggregated data; the break in the data graph line corresponds to the shift in the survey question in 1988.

Most of the Nannestad and Paldam (1991) Competency paper, however, is devoted to investigating sociotropic and egocentric effects at the micro level (that is, among individual Danish survey respondents), and to this end the three surveys taken during 1990-1991 (February and August, 1990 and

---

4. For an exposition, tailored to the logistic distribution, see Hibbs, 1987, chapter 5.
5. See Amemiya (1981), Amemiya (1985), chapter 9 and Maddala (1983), chapter 2.

%

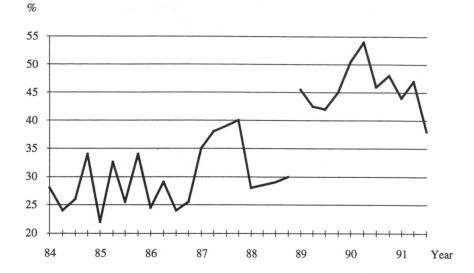

Figure 1. Competency Ratings of Danish Governments

February, 1991) were combined to form one large cross-section. Individual responses to questions about people's economic "situation" (retrospective and prospective) and economic "worries" were subjected to an orthogonal (Varimax) Factor Analysis, and three factors were identified; two are designated Sociotropic, one is designated Egocentric.[6] The Factors identified, which absorb about 55 percent of the variance in the constituent questions, were in turn used to create Factor Scores, that is, composite (and, because of the factor analysis method used, uncorrelated) Sociotropic and Egocentric variables. (See Table 3)

Nannestad and Paldam undertook a number of probit regression experiments to estimate the effects of the egocentric and sociotropic

---

6. Nannestad and Paldam use the term *egotropic*; as mentioned earlier, everywhere I prefer to use the term egocentric. The Factors/Factor Scores are given somewhat different names in the (1991) and (1992) papers, but they are identical.

SOLIDARITY OR EGOISM

Table 3
Questions Used to Form Nannestad and Paldam's Factor Scores in the 1990-1991 Cross-section

Egocentric/Personal Factor Scores	Sociotropic/National Factor Scores
Factor 1 *(Household Economy)*	*Factor 3* *(Worries About Social Problems)*

Personal economic situation,
  past and future
Household's Economic Situation,
  past and future
	Worry about social problem of
	  Unemployment
	Worry about social problem of
	  Inflation
	Worry about social problem of
	  Foreign Debt

Factor 2 *(Household Unemployment)*	
Household Unemployment, past and future Personal Unemployment, past	

Sources: Nannestad and Paldam (1991), table 4 and (1992), table 2.

motivations (as measured by the Factor Scores just described) on variation in the 1990-91 cross-section of respondents' binary ratings of government Competence. They concluded from the regression evidence that the two Egocentric factors dominate the Sociotropic one.

One problem with Nannestad and Paldam's basic research design, however, is that the sociotropic dimension is not well measured. The Sociotropic Factor Scores are based on responses to the question (translated from Danish, Nannestad and Paldam, 1991, Appendix A):

I shall now mention some social problems and ask you to be so kind as to tell me whether it is a problem which worries you 'a lot', 'only a little', or 'not at all' ... Unemployment .. Inflation/Price Increases .. Foreign Debt.

It simply is unclear to what extent that "worrying" about such economic problems, particularly unemployment and inflation problems, actually taps national-Sociotropic, as opposed to personal-Egocentric, concerns of Danish voters. At least to an outside, non-Danish analyst like myself, expressions of "worry" about unemployment and price increases, and for that matter even the size of the foreign debt, in opinion polls are just as likely to be based on self-interest as on public-interest, and for many people probably reflect some of each. On balance, however, Factor 3, especially by virtue of its unemployment and inflation components, might better be thought of as a third, perhaps weaker, Egocentric dimension than as a Sociotropic one.[7]

II.1 Voting Intentions, Competency Ratings and Sociotropic Motivations

Nannestad and Paldam's second paper (1992) parallels the first, except the dependent variable is a binary Bloc Vote intention,[8] rather than a binary Competency rating. Early on in this paper they discover that voters' assessments of the government's Competency (which in this paper is a five-point +1 to +5 score that exploits all the information in the survey responses) neutralizes almost all of the effects of the Egocentric and Sociotropic Factor Score variables in regression equations for Bloc Vote intentions (Nannestad and Paldam, 1992, Table 8). Conditioned on the five-point Competency rating variate, only the Factor 1 Egocentric variable

---

7. I discuss problems with the worry-based Sociotropic Factor Score further in chapter III.1 below.
8. Binary (Bourgeois Bloc/Socialist Bloc) codings of the question: "For what party would you vote if there were parliamentary elections tomorrow?" For the February and August 1990 polls a Bourgeois Bloc Vote intention is based on support for the Conservatives (KF), Agrarian Liberals (V) and the Radical Liberals (RV). In the February 1991 poll it is based on KF and V. The shift corresponds to the change in the party coalition comprising the Bourgeois government following the December 1990 election.

retains (attenuated, less significant) influence on Bloc Vote intention.[9] Consequently, Nannestad and Paldam sensibly propose the mediated Vote model (1992, Figure 1):

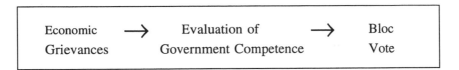

Figure 2. The Mediated Vote Model

It of course follows immediately from such a recursive chain that all results for government Competency ratings must pass through to Bloc Vote intentions (since the latter in reduced form is identical to the former), and by and large this is what Nannestad and Paldam find. (See Table 4)[10]

---

9. In related research, Goul Andersen (1992a, 1992b) also finds that voters' evaluations of the government's Competency, which he considers (rightly I think) to be a Sociotropic variable, exerts dominant statistical influence on "pragmatic confidence," that is, the electorate's confidence that the government will make "the right decisions for our country." I discuss the connections of Voting behavior to Competency assessments further in Chapter III.3 below.

10. The signs (+/-) of effects in Table 4 (and the source Tables) may be confusing. Contrary to convention, Nannestad and Paldam (1991) code the binary Competence variate as +1 for the negative position (low competency rating) and 0 for the positive position (high competency rating). And Nannestad and Paldam (1992) code the binary Vote variate as +1 for a vote intention in favor of the opposition (anti-government) and 0 as a vote intention in favor of the government. The fact that "most people in Denmark do not support the government" (1992, p.8), presumably in poll responses, is offered as an explanation for the coding of the Vote variable, but of course the sign coding of a dependent variable affects nothing but the coefficient signs of independent variables. In both the 1991 and 1992 papers Positive values of the Egocentric and Sociotropic Factor Scores represent *net* positive experiences or assessments concerning the Factor-analysis weighted constituent

Table 4

Probit Point Estimates of Egocentric and Sociotropic Effects on Competency Ratings and Vote Intentions for Danish Bourgeois Governments, 1990-1991 Cross-Section

Factors	Competence 1 = Negative, 0 = Positive	Vote Intention 1 = Anti-Government 0 = Pro-Government
Factor 1, Egocentric (Household Economy)	-0.328	-0.408
Factor 2, Egocentric (Household Unemployment)	-0.138	-0.149
Factor 3, Sociotropic (Social Problems "Worries")	-0.125	-0.075

Sources: Vote, Nannestad and Paldam (1992), table 3; Competence, Nannestad and Paldam (1991), table 5.

Yet, the reason so much of the earlier literature concluded that sociotropic motivation is what drives political behavior is precisely that variables measuring the electorate's perceptions of the government's capability in managing national problems exerted dominant influence in statistical analyses of survey data on voting behavior. In the founding papers of the sociotropic school (Kinder and Kiewet, 1979; 1981), to cite prominent examples, the fact that "party competence" assessments — responses to questions in the form "Do you think that the problems of [inflation, unemployment] would be handled better by the Democrats, by the Republicans, or about the same by both?" — dominated personal economic

questions, Negative values represent the opposite. The qualification "net," is important, as I show below.

grievance items in regression experiments[11] was taken to be the main evidence in favor of a sociotropic interpretation of American voting behavior.

As Kramer (1983) put it is his famous critique of cross-section estimates of sociotropic voting (about which I have much more to say later):

The most persuasive evidence for sociotropic voting lies not in the nonfindings concerning the role of personal economic circumstances .. but in .. findings common to several studies showing that individuals' voting decisions are ... related to ... assessments of how successfully the government is *handling economic problems* or of which party is more *competent in economic affairs*.... (Kramer, 1983, p. 103, emphasis added)

Viewed in the light of the original US conceptions of sociotropic motivation, Nannestad and Paldam's Competency variable — which is based on voters' assessments of the government's "ability to manage and solve problems" — would seem to be a much better measure of sociotropic concern than their "social problem worries" Factor Score. By this interpretation, Nannestad and Paldam (1992) demonstrate right off the bat, so to speak, that sociotropic orientations largely govern the Bloc Voting behavior of Danes.

At the same time, however, their evidence suggests that personal economic concerns (subject to the strong reservations developed in detail ahead) seem to affect Competency evaluations of the government, as more specific sociotropic evaluations might also, if properly measured. Indeed, Nannestad and Paldam's mediated Vote model, reproduced above in Figure 2, is a subset of the graph-model proposed by Kinder and Kiewet in their very first paper. (Kinder and Kiewet, 1979, figure 2, top frame)

Yet a multi-equation set-up, in which specific egocentric and sociotropic concerns drive more general evaluation of government competence, and general competence in turn has dominant proximate influence on voting behavior, takes us into the murky waters of trying to judiciously apply

---

11. In analyses of reported voting behavior in the U.S., such hypothetical "party competence" variables invariably dominated other sociotropic variables based on perceptions of national economic conditions and the government's success in dealing with them. In my view, however, the US competency questions come too close to being another way of measuring the vote itself.

political science theory and econometric practice to sort out the plausible joint endogeneities. Morris Fiorina struggled with these issues for some years, and offered the following summary advice:

Mediated Retrospective Evaluations reflect the economic conditions experienced and/or perceived by the citizen .... it is not terribly useful to compare their statistical strength with that of any particular individual experience. [citation to Kinder and Kiewet] To compare the statistical influence of personal financial situation with that of government economic performance [competence] is to compare a single ingredient to a complex product. (Fiorina, 1981, pp. 120-21)

This judgment seems as sound to me now as it did when first offered some dozen years ago. In any case, Nannestad and Paldam's Competency (1991) and Bloc Vote intentions (1992) papers are best considered as a piece, and I do so throughout the remainder of this monograph.

In order to probe the Danish and related international research more deeply, however, it is necessary to establish some relatively simple propositions from the pure theory of electoral choice and the econometrics of aggregation and specification error. I do this in the next sections, showing at various points along the way the relevance of the results established to the procedures and conclusions of Nannestad and Paldam and related empirical literature on sociotropic and egocentric motivations of political opinion and behavior.

III.

A Brief Exegesis of the Pure Theory of Electoral Choice and Political Valuation: Implications for Disentangling Sociotropic and Egocentric Political Motivations

Consider a two-party or two-bloc electoral system. Let U^I_{it} and U^O_{it} denote the utility associated by voter i at time t with the current incumbent party and the current opposition party, respectively. (Incumbent and opposition party may, of course, be replaced by supportive and non-supportive political choices more generally.) Although everything to follow could be generalized to the multi-party (or multi-choice) case, I confine this brief exposition to the two party/two bloc/two case, because the notation is a little less cluttered to work with, and because most of the literature in any event focuses on binary (mostly voting) political choices.

The probability (P) that utility maximizing voters will support the current incumbent party, $P(V_{it}=1)$, is simply the probability that U^I_{it} exceeds U^O_{it}:

$$(1) \qquad P\ (V_{it}=1) = P\ (U^I_{it}\text{-}U^O_{it}) > 0.$$

Let X^I, X^O denote a matrix of variables (voter perceptions of personal and national economic conditions and the government's responsibility for them, etc.), with associated parameter vector ß, that determines voter utility, and let voters be risk neutral so that U^I and U^O can be written as linear functions of X^I, X^O. Assume also for present purposes that utility is based wholly on retrospective evaluations, such that political valuations are based on a weighted average of current and past performance perceptions, with recent events given greater weight than earlier ones.

Retrospective valuation will prevail, for example, if voters use the experience of the present and discounted past to make judgments about the future, or if voters rationally want to attenuate the adverse effects of government "moral hazard" (emphasized by Peltzman, 1990) and, therefore, use old information in making current judgments, just the way insurance companies and governments often do when setting premiums ("experience ratings").

Given these basic assumptions, party utility differences are[1]

$$(2) \qquad U^I_{it} - U^O_{it} = \beta' \ r/(1+r) \sum_{j=0}^{\infty} 1/ (1+r)^j (X^I - X^O)_{it-j} + (w^I - w^O)_{it}$$

$$= \beta' \ (1-\delta) \sum_{j=0}^{\infty} \delta^j X_{it-j} + w_{it} \ ,$$

where $w_{it} = (w^I - w^O)_{it}$ are random shocks (idiosyncratic biases or events) advantaging the incumbent party at time t, $X_{it} = (X^I - X^O)_{it}$ is the perceived performance differential, and the discount rate r is > 0, so that the discount weight δ is < 1. The exponentially decaying weight scheme for retrospective evaluations (which corresponds to a "backward" present value) may be made much more general, but not without greater complication, which I shall avoid here.

Note that the upper limit of the summation (the most distant date of retrospective evaluation) is written as $j = \infty$, but this just should be interpreted as the "beginning of political life". (It could have been written as any finite date in the past and, with some occasional additional complication, all results to follow would pass through.) Notice also that for X held at some constant value, say X^p, the utility difference in (2) converges to $\beta'X^p$.

In most research settings, actual performance (as opposed to issue positions) is of course observed only for the incumbent party or bloc. In the absence of relevant data from surveys, the unobserved "shadow" performance of opposition parties must be assumed to be constant (which may move through time, as in Hibbs, 1987a, chapter 5 and Hibbs, 1987b, chapters 5, 7, 8 and 10) or might be set to some estimable fraction ($<$ or $>$ 1.0) of observed performance under the governing party/parties.[2] Economic models of voting and related political choices always do this at least

---

1. I assume, although this may easily be relaxed, that the X's are weighted by common parameters, ß and r, over all voters.
2. One of the great advantages of properly devised opinion survey studies is that investigators can directly ask voters about their perceptions of in-party versus out-party capacities and (actual and shadow) performance.

implicitly, unless one takes the highly implausible view that voters' conception of the opposition party's shadow performance is irrelevant to electoral choice.

Given equation (2), Vote (or other binary choice) probabilities from (1) may be written

$$(3) \qquad P\ (V_{it}=1) = P\ [\beta'\ (1-\delta) \sum_{j=0}^{\infty} \delta^j X_{it-j}] > w_{it}$$

$$\dot{=} F\ [\beta'\ (1-\delta) \sum_{j=0}^{\infty} \delta^j X_{it-j}],$$

where F is the cumulative distribution of random shocks w. If the w_{it} are distributed in bell-shaped fashion, then the natural choices for F are the cumulative standard normal (used by Nannestad and Paldam) and cumulative logistic functions.

III.1 Political Valuation in Denmark: Are Sociotropic Effects Nil?

An important message of equations (1)-(3) is that the ß parameters should always be interpreted as the weight placed on voters' assessment of performance *differentials* (in-parties versus out-parties) with respect to some set of performance variables (X's). This means, for example, that unfavorable developments in variables of concern to voters would be expected to yield a deterioration in support for (or Competency ratings of) the government *only* if voters judge that the situation would have been even worse under the opposition.[3]

In this connection, consider the evidence in Tables 3 and 4 of Nannestad and Paldam (1992), which I have excerpted from to create Table 5 below.

In the first panel (a) of Table 5, I summarize Nannestad and Paldam's probit regression results for the response of individual Bloc Voting intentions to Egocentric and Sociotropic orientations, as measured by the

---

3. Readers averse to analytical representations no doubt will observe (correctly!) that one hardly needs the simple algebra of equations (1)-(3) to convey this obvious point. Hopefully the mathematics to come will deliver more value added.

Table 5

Egocentric and Sociotropic Effects on Bloc Voting Intentions in Denmark, 1990-1991 Cross-Section

a) Estimates From Probit Regression with Factor Scores

Personal/Egocentric Factors	*National/Sociotropic Factors*
Household Economy	Social Problem Worries
−0.408	−0.075 (NS)
Household Unemployment	
−0.149	

b) Estimates From Probit Regressions with Egocentric Factor Scores, and Social Problem "Worry" Variables Considered One at a Time

Personal/Egocentric Factors	National/Sociotropic Variables
	Unemployment Worry
	−0.148
Coefficients ≈ to 1st panel	Inflation Worry
above in every regression	−0.141
	Foreign Debt Worry
	+0.111

Sources: a) Nannestad and Paldam (1992), table 3; b) (1992), table 4.
Notes: NS = not significant; unless so noted, variables are significant at 0.05 or better. Dependent variable is Vote intention, coded +1 for opposition vote, 0 for government vote.

Factor Scores discussed earlier. The Egocentric variables are highly significant statistically and, at least potentially, have real substantive clout. For example, Nannestad and Paldam's estimates imply that an unfavorable change of one unit (which in the Factor Scores corresponds to one standard deviation) in general household economic grievances and household unemployment grievances would together yield a decline in the Vote for the government bloc of about 21 percentage points.[4] By contrast, the Socio-tropic factor is estimated to have a small and statistically insignificant effect.

These regression estimates lead Nannestad and Paldam to conclude that "contrary to the Kinder and Kiewet result we find that in Denmark personal grievances seem to have the most significant impact on the probability of an anti-government vote" (1992, p. 10). As in Kinder and Kiewet's work and that of others who have studied micro cross-sectional data, such conclusions must be carefully interpreted. They pertain to the dispersion across individuals at a given point in time, and as such tell us nothing about the sources of actual electoral change.

The 21 percentage point effect computed above, for example, is far larger than any inter-election Bloc Vote shift ever observed. (See Chapter III.3 below on the sluggishness of Scandinavian bloc voting.) Implied Egocentric effects of this scale, on both Voting behavior and Competency ratings (see Table 6), are evidently what prompted Goul Andersen (1992) to remark that the aggregate magnitude of personal economic assessments in Denmark have exhibited relatively little time variation since 1984, and therefore are unlikely to have produced more than modest movements in aggregate Competency ratings, Voting outcomes and the like. Hence, although variations of one standard deviation exist across individuals in a given survey sample, they are not accurate guides to the magnitudes of movements through time in the underlying sources of political choice or to the magnitudes of aggregate voting changes.

Additional estimations reported by Nannestad and Paldam show that the Sociotropic Factor's constituent "worry" variables, considered individually, each exert significant and substantively important influence on the Vote intentions.[5] An excerpt from these results is shown in the second panel (b) of my Table 5. According to these estimates, one-unit unfavorable

---

4. Marginal effects on P(V) implied by Probit coefficient estimates, say for variable X_k, $\partial F(\text{ß}'X)/\partial X_k$, are given by $f(\text{ß}'X) \cdot \text{ß}_k$, where $F(\text{ß}'X)$ is the cumulative standard normal (the Probit function evaluated), f is the standard normal density, and ß_k is the Probit coefficient estimate of the X variable of interest. I evaluated $f(\text{ß}'X)$ at the means of X (that is, at the value of the constant since Factor scores have zero mean) to compute $\partial F(\text{ß}'X)/\partial X_k$.

5. The "worry" variables evidently are not highly inter-correlated, and so it would have been more revealing had Nannestad and Paldam reported a joint regression with all three included together.

movements in unemployment and inflation "worries" would be expected to yield a decline in Voting intentions for the government of 9 to 10 percentage points.[6]

As is clear from Table 5, and as Nannestad and Paldam themselves tell us, the only reason the Sociotropic Factor was insignificant in the top panel regressions (and similar regressions throughout their Vote and, presumably, Competence papers) was that the Foreign Debt worry variable affects Voting intentions with sign (positive) opposite to those of the Unemployment and Inflation worry variables. Consequently, when combined (literally added up after weighting) to form a common Factor Score, the effects of the worry variables tend to cancel, thereby driving the Sociotropic Factor Score coefficient to zero.

As I emphasized in the exposition of the theory of rational electoral choice, however, there is no reason in the world why rational voters should not gravitate toward a Conservative government when Foreign Debt "worries" loom large in their minds, as long as Conservative governments are viewed as more competent and attentive to such issues than the Socialist opposition.[7] Indeed, Nannestad and Paldam make the very same point (1992, note 17), and observe that Bourgeois governments in the 1980s attached higher priority than the Socialist opposition to the foreign debt issue, and succeeded in making substantial progress on it. Yet, they do not draw the logical implication that the quite rational Bloc Vote responses to debt worries by their survey respondents means that the Foreign Debt question should not have been combined with the Inflation and Unemployment questions to form a common Sociotropic Factor score, no matter what loadings for the items were obtained via orthogonal Varimax rotations.

III.2 OLS and Probit Estimation: Theory and Practice

I return now to empirical applications of the basic retrospective choice function of equation (3). If the random shocks w_{it} conform to the normal or logistic density functions, and there are either many observations (indexed, say, by t) on V for each configuration of X_{it} ("many observations per cell")

---

6. In the absence of a multivariate regression it is not possible to compute the estimated effects of a joint movement with precision.
7. In some of the US literature, such behavior is known as "policy voting" (for example, Kiewet 1981, 1983).

or one is working with aggregated data (for example, group averages or aggregate time series), then $F^{-1}V_t$ is readily found and least squares[8] may be applied to

$$(4) \qquad F^{-1}V_t = \beta' \, (1-\delta) \sum_{j=0}^{\infty} \delta^j X_{t-j}.$$

In the case of the logistic (which differs trivially from the normal and is easier to work with), $F^{-1}V_t = \log[V_t/(1-V_t)]$ and is known as a "logit." In the case of the normal, $F^{-1}V_t$ is just the inverse cumulative normal (which is easy to compute numerically but has no explicit form), and is known as a "probit."

Among the advantages, in terms of realism, of taking choice theory seriously is that predictions from logit and probit models of $P(V_{it})$ and $P(V_t)$, in contrast to those from unconstrained least squares set-ups, can never fall outside the 0,1 interval. Moreover, when utility/performance differentials are zero, and so neither party (or neither choice) is evaluated as being better than the other, the systematic prediction from logits and probits is always $P(V_{it})=1/2$; the vote-choice outcome is a toss up.

Alternatively, if one assumes that w_{it} are distributed uniformly over some finite interval at each period — say between $a+d_t$ and $b+d_t$, $a<b$ — then least squares may be applied directly to equations in the form of (3) and the F function just scales all parameters on the right-side by $1/(b-a)$. (See Fair, 1978) Though in pure theory unrealistic, this is by far the most common (but usually implicit) assumption in the aggregate economics and voting literature. On the other hand, researchers working with political choice data typically report that least squares (or the so-called linear probability model) yields estimation results that are substantively indistinguishable (up to a scalar of transformation) from those generated by logit and probit algorithms.[9]

---

8. In this case Nonlinear Least Squares by virtue of the backward discounting scheme.
9. In the interval $0.3 < P(V) < 0.7$, probit and logit estimation yields results essentially identical to OLS. And, no matter what the true distribution function of the errors, least squares is consistent, whether applied to micro or macro data.

A pertinent example in the present context is supplied by Nannestad and Paldam's estimates for Egocentric and Sociotropic influences on Danish voters' ratings of the government's Competency in the 1990-1991 combined cross-section described in Chapter II (Table 6).

The Competency variable in Nannestad and Paldam's OLS regression in Table 6 exploits the full range of responses in the survey question and, therefore, may be compared directly to the Probit estimates without adjustment for the scalar of transformation.[10] Except for sign changes produced by different sign-codings of the Competency variable from one paper to the other, Nannestad and Paldam's OLS results are indeed very similar to their probit results. And what little difference there is may stem from the slightly larger size of the Probit sample.

Henceforth I shall therefore assume that we operate in a linear probability world, or in a setting where $F^{-1}V_t$ may be computed directly, and just write V_{it} and X_{it} rather than $F^{-1}V_t$ or $F(X,\beta)$ and so on. Among other things, this makes it much easier to establish precise aggregation and measurement (specification) bias results, which are particularly relevant to the evaluation of research on sociotropic and egocentric motivations of political behavior.

III.3 Electoral Dynamics, Lag Regressions and the Sluggishness of Scandinavian Bloc Voting

Regressions including lagged endogenous (dependent) variables are sometimes used to make dynamic inferences about the evolution of political opinions and behavior. (Nannestad and Paldam call such equations the "change version" of their models.) To explore the implications of such models in the present context, consider the basic political choice function of equation (4) after backward iteration for one, and then N, periods. These dynamic solutions yield

(5a) $\qquad V_{it} = \delta \, V_{it-1} + \beta' \, (1-\delta) \, X_{it-1},$

---

10. In other words, since the dependent variable is coded 1 to 5 rather than 0,1 (binary), the OLS dependent variable can be thought of as a crude approximation to $F^{-1}V$ of equation 4 (the case of uniformly distributed stochastic shocks).

Table 6

OLS and Probit Estimates of Egocentric and Sociotropic Effects on the Competency Ratings of Danish Bourgeois Governments, 1990-1991 Cross-section

	Estimation Method	
	Coefficient Estimate	Effect of -1σ Change on P(V=1)
Factor	*OLS*	*Probit*
Factor 1, Egocentric (Household Economy)	0.342 | 0.10	0.328 | 0.13
Factor 2, Egocentric (Household Unemployment)	0.133 | 0.04	0.138 | 0.05
Factor 3, Sociotropic (Social Problem "Worries")	0.099 | 0.03	0.125 | 0.05

Sources: OLS, Nannestad and Paldam (1992), table 9, N = 1031; Probit, Nannestad and Paldam (1991), table 5, N = 1080.

Notes: In the OLS regression (and throughout Nannestad and Paldam, 1992) the Competency variate exploits the full information in the 1990-91 surveys and is coded +1 for Great Distrust, +2 for Distrust, +3 for Neither, +4 for Trust and +5 for Great Trust concerning the "government's ability to solve problems." In the Probit regression (here, in Table 4 and throughout Nannestad and Paldam, 1991) the Competency variate is coded +1 for Negative assessments (corresponding to codes +1 and +2 above) and 0 for Positive assessments (corresponding to codes +3, +4 and +5 above). Effects of -1σ changes for the Probit estimates are $f(a)\text{'}\beta_k$, where a is the intercept constant and f the normal density, and for the OLS estimates are based on the assumption that the Competency scores are normally distributed with mean of 2.874 and σ of 1.12 (Nannestad and Paldam's estimates).

$$(5b) \qquad V_{it} = \delta^N V_{it\text{-}N} + \beta\text{'} (1-\delta) \sum_{j=0}^{N-1} \delta^j X_{it\text{-}j} ,$$

for individual micro relations and, after aggregation,

(6a) $\quad \bar{V}_t = \delta \, \bar{V}_{t-1} + \text{ß'} \, (1-\delta) \, \bar{X}_{t-1},$

(6b) $\quad \bar{V}_t = \delta^N \, \bar{V}_{t-N} + \text{ß'} \, (1-\delta) \sum_{j=0}^{N-1} \delta^j \, \bar{X}_{t-j},$

for macro level relations.

Equations (5)-(6) comprise the theoretical basis of the time series and cross-section "lag" analyses undertaken by Nannestad and Paldam, and by many others. Perhaps the most important thing to notice is that as the time preference parameter δ approaches 1.0 (that is, as the discount rate, r, that voters apply to past performance differentials goes to infinity), political choices (V) evolve according to random walk (plus moving average error which, as noted above, I have omitted).

Evidence in Nannestad and Paldam's work, and from comparable research on Sweden, suggests that Scandinavian Bloc Voting behavior, at least as recorded in polls, is extremely sluggish, implying a very low rate of discounting of the past (and/or anticipated future). I summarize some of the evidence in Table 7.

The Danish estimates in the top panel of Table 7 are based on current (hypothetical election) Bloc Vote intentions, and actual Bloc Votes in the most recent (last) election as "recalled" by respondents in the 1990 and 1991 surveys commissioned by Nannestad and Paldam. Peter Nannestad has suggested to me (in private conversation) that such "recall" data may well give a somewhat exaggerated picture of the true stability of Bloc Voting.

However, Danish data in the middle panel of Table 7 on the stability of the Vote going to the core party of each Bloc — the Conservatives and Social Democrats — indicate that recall vote reports and panel vote reports (that is, reports of each respondent's voting behavior obtained at the time of each election) diverge only moderately. The stability of the vote for the Conservative and Socialist *Parties* will of course be substantially less than the vote for the Bourgeois and Socialist *Blocs* because voters are more reluctant to cross Bloc lines than to cross party lines within a Bloc. It is very likely, therefore, that Nannestad and Paldam's estimates of Bloc Voting stability are not far off the mark.

This inference is strengthened by data for Sweden in the bottom panel of the Table. The Swedish estimates are based partly on panel data and partly on recall data. Although, the panel and recall reports are not distinguished in Table 7, the Swedish principal investigator, Sören

Table 7
Stability of Voting in Denmark and Sweden: Probability of Current Vote Given Previous Vote

a) Denmark

Recall Data	**1990 Vote** (hypothetical election)	
1988 vote	Bourgeois Bloc	Socialist Bloc
Bourgeois Bloc	*0.96*	0.04
Socialist Bloc	0.03	*0.97*

Recall Data	**1987 Vote**	
1984 Vote	Conservatives	Social Democrats
Conservatives	0.84	NA
Social Democrats	NA	0.87

Panel Data	**1988 Vote**	
1987 Vote	Conservatives	Social Democrats
Conservatives	*0.74*	NA
Social Democrats	NA	*0.82*

b) Sweden

Recall and Panel Data	**1985 Vote**	
1988 vote	Bourgeois Bloc	Socialist Bloc
Bourgeois Bloc	*0.97*	0.03
Socialist Bloc	0.05	*0.95*

Sources: Denmark 1990: Nannestad and Paldam (1992), table 5; Denmark 1987-88: Tonsgaard, 1989, table 5.15; Sweden, Holmberg and Gilljam (1986), table 7.14; . For approximately one-third of the Danish respondents in the top panel data (Feb. 1991 survey) the current vote is hypothetical in 1991, and the lagged vote is recalled for the 12 December 1990 election.

Holmberg, informs me (in private conversation) that the stability of the "recalled" Bloc Vote generally exceeds that of the panel reports by only one-half to one percentage point.

All things considered, then, it seems highly probable that the great stability of the aggregate Bloc Vote from election to election in Scandinavia is in fact produced by great micro level inertia in the Bloc Voting allegiances of individual Bourgeois and Socialist voters, just as Table 7 implies. In terms of the more formal, rational retrospective model of equations (1)-(6), δ therefore must be very close to 1.0. This indeed (by necessity, given the data in the top panel of Table 7) is what Nannestad and Paldam find in a regression (analogous to my equation 5a) of the current Bloc Vote on the recalled Bloc Vote plus the Competency variable (scored from +1 for very negative to +5 for very positive) and all of the Factor Scores previously described.

Recalling that $P(V=1)$ is the probability of an opposition (anti-government) Vote, the probit regression yields (Nannestad and Paldam, 1992, Table 10):

(7) $P(V_{it}) = F [-0.033 + 3.371 V_{it-1} - 0.498$ Competency
   + Insignificant Egocentric and Sociotropic Factor Scores],

where F denotes the cumulative standard normal.

Translated to more familiar probabilities, these probit estimates imply the results shown in Table 8.

Table 8 reveals what for the most part is obvious from the stability of the Danish voting behavior shown in Table 7: Danish Bloc Voting outcomes (as measured by the surveys considered) evolve very nearly according to a random walk[11] perturbed by Competency "shocks," that is, by shifts in public perceptions of the government's management ability. As I argued earlier, such Competency shocks are probably best regarded as measuring movements in a *general* Sociotropic orientation.

Although Competency shocks disturb the stability of Bloc voting across any given pair of elections only a little (Table 8 shows the consequences of

---

11. Without drift, since the constant in equation 7 (−0.03) had a t-ratio of only 0.09 in Nannestad and Paldam's regression.

Table 8

Probability of a Vote for the Opposition Bloc (V_{it}) Given Previous Bloc Vote (V_{it-1}) and Competency Rating (Comp) of the Government, Denmark 1990-1991

Conditional Probabilities	$V_{it-1} = 1$	$V_{it-1} = 0$
Prob[(V_{it}=1)|Comp=$\hat{\mu}$+1$\hat{\sigma}$]	0.91	0.02
Prob[(V_{it}=1)|Comp=$\hat{\mu}$−1$\hat{\sigma}$]	0.99	0.18
Percentage of Electorate:	0.96	0.04

Note: Estimates computed from equation (7) in the text.

shifts of two standard deviations, which represents a huge Competency shock), their effects are very long lived among the small fraction of voters who actually are induced to cross Bloc lines.

The sources of shifts in the electorate's assessment of government Competency (the time path of which was graphed in Figure 1 above), therefore, is the place to look for specific Sociotropic and Egocentric effects on Danish voting outcomes. I now turn to this topic, which is most productively considered in the context of some standard results on the econometrics of measurement and specification error.

IV.
The Econometrics of Measurement Specification Error: A Useful General Result

Consider two linear multivariate regression régimes, the first being the "true" structure generating the outcomes in nature, and the second being the "estimated" structure which is contaminated by measurement and specification error:

(8) $\quad$ $V = XB + U$ $\quad$ ("true" structure)
(9) $\quad$ $V = ZC + E$ $\quad$ ("estimated" structure),

where $E(X'U) = E(Z'U) = 0$, and V denotes the dependent variable which I assume to be measured without error,[1] XB denotes the true matrix of variables and associated coefficients generating V, and ZC denotes the measured variables and coefficients used by the researcher to obtain empirical estimates. As will become obvious ahead, measurement error bias is readily converted to specification error bias, allowing us to use the standard linear algebra of the later to deduce the consequences of the former. Note that V, X, Z, U and E may be of any dimension in time and space (an aggregate time series, a micro cross-section, or a time series of cross-sections) and that the Z variables may be a subset of the X variables, a different matrix of (irrelevant) variables entirely, or some combination of the two.

Least squares estimation of (9) yields

---

1. If V is contaminated by measurement error that has zero covariance with specification and measurement errors in Z (which is normally the case), nothing to follow is affected. If errors of measurement in V and X are correlated, however, the right side of (9) should include an additional omitted variable corresponding to the error in measured V.

$$(10.1) \quad \hat{C} \quad = (Z' \, Z)^{-1} \, Z' \, V$$
$$(10.2) \quad\quad\quad = (Z' \, Z)^{-1} \, Z' \, XB + (Z' \, Z)^{-1} \, Z' \, U,$$

which gives in expectation

$$(11.1) \quad E(\hat{C}) \quad = (Z' \, Z)^{-1} \, Z' \, XB$$
$$(11.2) \quad\quad\quad = bB,$$

where b, is a matrix of coefficients from least squares projections (auxiliary regressions) of each variable (vector) in X on all variables (vectors) in Z.

Finally, letting ZC be of dimension j and XB of dimension k (as noted before j may be $\leq$, $\geq$, or $\neq$ k), we may express (11.1)-(11.2) in scalar notation as

$$(11.3) \quad E\,(\hat{C}_j) \quad = B_{k=j} + \Sigma_{k\neq j}B_k \cdot b_{kj} \, ,$$

for each $\hat{C}_j$.

Hence, the expected value of the coefficient estimate obtained by least squares algorithms for each independent variable in the misspecified ("estimation") model is equal to the corresponding true-structure parameter of that variable (which of course may be zero) plus the sum of the products of every other true-structure parameter times the coefficient from the conditional projection (partial regression slope) of each true-structure variable on all variables in the misspecified model.

Nearly all we need to know about the theoretical consequences of measurement and specification error for point estimation of egocentric and sociotropic effects on Voting intentions and government Competency ratings in the Nannestad and Paldam papers (or, for that matter, in others) can be obtained from appropriate application of equations (11.1)-(11.3). In the chapters to follow I flesh out this assertion with a number of examples inspired by the Danish research.

V.
Egocentric and Sociotropic Influences on Political Choices: The General Model in Space and Time

Let me begin with the incontestable assumption that Voting intentions, government Competency ratings and the like are based at least to some degree on both purely Personal ("egocentric") and purely National ("sociotropic") motivations, though one or the other may in principle dominate political life. Moreover, it must also be true that economically driven egocentric and sociotropic political behavior are based on voters' conception of the "politically relevant" components of personal economic experiences and perceptions of national economic conditions, rather than on how such economic events might be registered in official statistics and polling data.

In Kramer's (1983) famous paper on the topic, "politically relevant" economic events were confined by assumption to outcomes that could plausibly be traced to government action or inaction. Hence, voters would neither reward governments for personal windfalls originating with, say, lottery winnings and inheritances, nor punish governments for the macroeconomic consequences of events, say, like the OPEC energy price hikes. Though logical, Kramer's assumption that only government induced economic events are "politically relevant" is unnecessarily restrictive. Here I take politically relevant to mean all components of perceived personal and national economic events that motivate political behavior, although at several points I will draw out the implications of assumptions about likely relative magnitudes for (mis)estimation of true Sociotropic and Egocentric effects.

Finally, note that even though attention focuses exclusively on economic events, personal and national economic assessments will in general be multidimensional. For simplicity, and with very little loss to the generality of the points I wish to make, however, I shall treat them as unidimensional.

With these points in mind, I can now write general models. Let the politically relevant component of voter i's assessment of his/her Personal economic well-being at time t be denoted P^*_{it}, and let the corresponding measured assessment (by opinion poll surveys, etc.) be denoted P_{it}, such that

$$(12) \qquad P_{it} \quad = P^*_{it} + e_{p,it} \, ,$$

where e are random measurement errors, distributed so that $Cov\ (e_p, P^*) = 0$.

Analogously, let individual assessments of the politically relevant component of National economic well-being be denoted N^* and let the corresponding measured assessments be denoted N, such that

$$(13) \qquad N_{it} \quad = N^*_{it} + e_{n,it} \, ,$$

where $Cov(e_n, P^*) = 0$. Remember that e_n and e_p include not just pure measurement error in survey instruments, but all components of Personal and National economic well-being that voters deem irrelevant to political valuation.

Nearly all of the literature uses models linear or linearizable in the parameters, and so I maintain that (very convenient) assumption here. A general linear model for the response of voters' political choices to assessments of Personal and National economic conditions may therefore be written over voters i and times t (that is, over time and space) as

$$(14) \qquad V_{it} \quad = ß_1\ P^*_{it} + ß_2\ N^*_{it} + u_{it} \, ,$$

where u is a variable representing all other variables affecting Voting, Competency ratings and so on. For my purposes there is no harm in assuming that $Cov\ (u, P^*) = Cov\ (u, N^*) = 0$, although this will not in general be true for models as restrictive as (14). Indeed the consequences of such covariances, where u was taken to represent partisan predispositions, played an important role in Kramer's (1983) article, and has been the object of a large literature on partisanship-mediated political evaluation.[1]

Take equation (14), then, to be the true structure generating V over all

---

1. See, for example, Fiorina (1981). For Scandinavia — U.S. comparisons, see Granberg and Holmberg (1986).

i and t. Aggregating over voters at each time t, we obtain the true time series model

$$(15.1) \quad \bar{V}_t = ß_1 \overline{P^*}_t + ß_2 \overline{N^*}_t + \bar{u}_t .$$

And, at any time t, the true cross-section model is

$$(15.2) \quad V_i = ß_1 P^*_i + ß_2 N^*_i + u_i .$$

I now apply these abstract results to Nannestad and Paldam's empirical results for Denmark.

VI.
Competence Assessments of Danish Governments: Macroeconomic Results

As I noted in chapter II, in the first part of their 1991 paper Nannestad and Paldam investigate the relation of aggregate percentage Competency ratings of Danish Bourgeois Governments over 1983-1991 to a number of macroeconomic variables. Although much of the variance in the government Competency time series is due to a shift in question wording in 1988 (see Figure 1 above and Nannestad and Paldam, 1991, Tables 1-3), some significant macroeconomic effects are identified. I abstract from the relevant regressions in Table 9.

The significant macroeconomic coefficients in these regressions, particularly those pertaining to changes in the inflation rate and the real wages growth rate, are interpreted by Nannestad and Paldam to be evidence of egocentric political behavior (the importance of "private [personal] economic conditions," 1991, pages 25 and 30). Yet common sense, which I dress up in econometric formalities just below, clearly informs us that no such conclusion can be drawn from their aggregate regression evidence. The macroeconomic analyses, though intrinsically of interest to the study of economics and politics, simply cannot distinguish Egocentric from Sociotropic motivations of political behavior.

In terms of the true aggregate time series model of equation (15.1) which permits both Personal and National economic conditions to exert influence, just what do Nannestad and Paldam's time series estimates yield? With no loss of important generality, we may express their macroeconomic regressions as unidimensional experiments of the form

$$(16) \qquad \bar{V}_t \qquad = c\, \bar{X}_t + e_t \,,$$

where represents $\bar{X}$ (economy-wide, average) macroeconomic variables. Applying the results of (11.1)-(11.3) to (15.1) and (16), we see that

$$(17) \qquad E(\hat{c}) = \text{\ss}_1 b \overline{P^*}\, \bar{X} + \text{\ss}_2 \bar{b} \overline{N^*} \bar{X}$$

Table 9

Percentage of the Public Expressing Negative Assessments of the Competence of Danish Bourgeois Governments (V_t), Macroeconomic Time Series 1983-1991

	Regressions	
Independent Variables	*(1)*	*(2)*
Change of Inflation Rate	2.89	NA
Change of Real Wage Growth Rate	NA	-1.82
Change of Unemployment Rate (narrow conception)	0.83	0.87
Change of Balance of Payments	NS	NS

Sources: Nannestad and Paldam (1991), tables 1 and 3.

---

where, as noted earlier, the b's are equivalent to slopes from auxiliary regressions of $\overline{p}^*$ on $\overline{X}$ and $\overline{N}^*$ on $\overline{X}$, respectively. Both of these slopes should lie in the interval 0,1. If voters' assessments of the politically relevant component of macroeconomic outcomes closely follows actual developments in economy-wide aggregates, $b\overline{N^*X}$ may be quite close to 1.0; in any case it will almost surely will be larger than the corresponding personal effects projection, $b\overline{P^*X}$.[1]

---

1. In US aggregate data for presidential election years from 1956 to 1980, the regression of average responses to a "family finances over the last year" question (P), coded +1 for "better," 0 for "same" and −1 for "worse," on percentage changes in aggregate real personal disposable income yields a slope of about 0.5, an intercept of about 0.0 and a correlation of 0.68. The same regression with means from an identically coded "national business conditions" question (N) yielded a correlation of 0.91 and slope closer to 0.8. (Kiewet, 1983, p. 134; and my computation from Rivers and Kiewet, 1985, p. 216.) The corresponding slopes for average P^* and N^* (the bivariate regressions of unobserved, average true egocentric effects and average true

The main conclusion, however, is that Nannestad and Paldam's macroeconomic regressions (1991, Table 1) are of no help in estimating the relative importance of egocentric and sociotropic political motivation. Instead, the coefficients register an attenuated sum of both Personal (Egocentric) and National (Sociotropic) effects.

---

sociotropic effects on aggregate income changes) would likely be smaller, but in this case of time series models not dramatically so because the errors (deviations of P^* from P and N for N^*) will tend to cancel out after aggregation. See the following chapter.

VII.
Cross-Section Evidence on Sociotropic and Egocentric Influences on Political Behavior: Norway and Sweden

Most of Nannestad and Paldam's empirical evidence for the dominance of Egocentric motivations in explaining Danish political behavior, which I summarized in Tables 4-6 above, is based on cross-sectional analysis of 1990-1991 poll data. How do their results compare to evidence available for Norway and Sweden — countries that have much in common with Denmark. Tables 10 and 11 summarize, in a very abbreviated fashion, estimates of Sociotropic and Egocentric effects that were reported in a range of studies I reviewed.

The Norwegian data (Table 10) exhibit a mixed pattern. During the 1970s and 1980s, voters' "Trust" in government seems to have been more responsive to Personal economic experiences than assessments of the government's National economic performance. These results broadly resemble those obtained by Nannestad and Paldam for trust in the government's management Competence. If one takes the Danish and Norwegian results at face value (which I do not), then when it comes to voters' assessments of the trustworthiness and competence of governments, Egocentric motivation may not be unique to Denmark in the Nordic area.

There is also some evidence of Egocentric motivation in Norwegian Voting behavior, in particular in 1985. However, when the Sociotropic questions pertain to which party is "best," or are confined to those respondents who view government as the "cause" of unfavorable macro-economic outcomes, National economic orientations clearly dominate Personal ones.

The evidence for Sweden, summarized in Table 11, implies that Sociotropic motivation clearly dominates reported Voting behavior. The results, therefore, contrast with those obtained for Denmark by Nannestad and Paldam, but are consistent with earlier results, obtained mainly during the first half of the 1980s, for the United States and, by greatly varying degrees, for some other countries. (See chapter I.)

Table 10

Norway: Cross-Sectional Evidence on Egocentric and Sociotropic Effects on Political Choices (Absolute Values of Significant, Properly Signed Coefficients)

Trust in Government (Listhaug, 1989 Table 10.11, OLS)	*Egocentric* (Personal Finances)	*Sociotropic* (Gov't Performance on Unemployment, Inflation)
1973	0.196	NS
1977	0.108	NS
1981	0.076	0.08
1985	0.069	NS

Remarks: Coefficients were conditioned on partisanship and ideology.

Vote Intention (Miller and Listhaug (1984, Table 4, OLS))	*Personal Finances*	*Party Best on Unemp., Inflation* (sum of Coeffs)
1969	NS	0.3
1977	NS	0.42
1981	0.13	0.42

Remarks: The coefficients are standardized "betas" and were conditioned on partisanship and ideology. The authors note that personal (egocentric) effects may be reflected in (and absorbed by) the "party best" responses. The "party best" question may also be a noisy measure of the vote itself.

Bloc Vote Intention (Listhaug, 1989a, 1989b Tables 7.1-7.2, Probit)	*Personal Finances*	*National Economy*
1985 (a)	0.821	0.57
1985 (b)	NS	NS
	Government Cause of Unemp., Inflation 0.508	
	Inflation Higher Under Opposition 0.568	

Remarks: Estimates in (a) were conditioned only on partisanship. Estimates in (b) were conditioned on many controls and, as shown, government attribution variables.

Table 11

Sweden: Cross-Sectional Evidence on Egocentric and Sociotropic Effects on Political Choices (Absolute Values of Significant Properly Signed Coefficients)

Bloc Vote	Egocentric	Sociotropic
	Personal Economic Development	Judgment of Bloc's Economy Policy
1984 (standardized OLS)	0.07	0.66
	Personal Economic Development	Judgment of National Economy
1985 (OLS)	NS	0.22
	Personal Economic Development	Judgment of Party Responsibility for National Economy
1991 (OLS)	NS	0.86
Vote Change 1988-91	NS	0.45

Remarks: Sociotropic effects dominate, even with controls for ideology and partisanship, and are much enlarged when the question focuses on party/bloc responsibility for the national economy (1991).

Notes: NS = not significant.

Sources: Holmberg (1984), figure 5.1; Holmberg and Gilljam (1985), figure 7.2; Gilljam and Holmberg (1992), figure 16.1

As in the Norwegian data, Sociotropic effects in Sweden are magnified substantially when respondents were asked to respond in terms of Party-Government *responsibility* for national economic developments. (Unfortunately, no such responsibility filter targeted on Personal economic experiences was incorporated in the survey design.) This feature of the results in Tables 10 and 11 clearly illustrates the basic methodological argument of chapters 4 and 5: The statistical influence of economic experiences and assessments recorded by surveys (here sociotropic, but in principle both sociotropic and egocentric) to political opinion and behavior is much stronger when the politically relevant component (the government responsibility filter) is explicitly measured.

The cross-sectional evidence on the relative importance of Egocentric and Sociotropic political motivation — obtained at various dates, for various political choices and for different countries — thus yields quite a mixed and unstable message. Some of the instability obviously stems from variations across (and sometimes within) studies in the survey questions taken to represent Personal and, especially National, economic variables. Indeed, I argued earlier that Nannestad and Paldam's "Worry" variables were poor measures of Sociotropic orientation, and I also pointed out that their Competency variable bears close resemblance to the most robust Sociotropic variables in the research of Kinder and Kiewet on the United States, Goul Andersen on Denmark, and others.

Moreover, as Kramer (1983) first taught us, cross-sectional research on economic motivations for voting choices is especially prone to mis-measurement of the politically relevant components of economic perceptions and experience, and this too can lead to erroneous conclusions about the relative importance of Sociotropic and Egocentric effects on political attitudes and behavior. In the next chapter I develop the particulars, with special reference to Nannestad and Paldam's work on Denmark.

VIII.
Inferences from Cross-sectional Regressions: Implications of Egocentric and Sociotropic Influence on Danish Political Behavior

As earlier, derivations will be obtained for unidimensional specifications of Personal (Egocentric) and National (Sociotropic) variables. This simplification reduces the estimation issues I wish to focus on to essentials, with hardly any loss to the generality of my results. Hence, the cross-section models used by Nannestad and Paldam, and many others, can be expressed in simplified fashion as

$$(18) \qquad V_i \qquad = c_1 P_i + c_2 N_i + e_i \ ,$$

whereas, the true cross-sectional model of equation (15.2), after substitution from equations (12)-(13), is

$$(19) \qquad V_i \qquad = \beta_1 (P_i - e_{pi}) + \beta_2 (N_i - e_{ni}) + u_i \ .$$

It immediately follows from equations (11.1)-(11.3) that the regressions undertaken by Nannestad and Paldam yield in expected value

$$(20.1) \qquad E (\hat{c}_1) = \beta_1 - \beta_1 \, be_p P.N - \beta_2 \, be_n P.N$$

for Personal/Egocentric effects, and

$$(20.2) \qquad E (\hat{c}_2) = \beta_2 - \beta_2 \, be_n N.P - \beta_1 \, be_p N.P \ ,$$

for National/Sociotropic effects.

Nannestad and Paldam use orthogonal Egocentric and Sociotropic Factor Scores as independent variables in their models (See Section II), and so the P and N variables have zero covariance. Consequently, the partial slopes $be_p P.N$ and $be_n N.P$ are identical to the corresponding bivariate slopes, $be_p P$

and be_nN, and the partial slopes $be_nP.N$ and $be_pN.P$ are zero.[1] Hence, the expected value of estimates obtained from the simplified Nannestad and Paldam set-up reduce to

$$(21.1) \quad E\ (\hat{c}_1) = \beta_1 - \beta_1\ r(e_p,P) \cdot Se_p/Sp$$

for Egocentric (P^*) effects, and

$$(21.2) \quad E\ (\hat{c}_2) = \beta_2 - \beta_2\ r(e_n,N) \cdot Se_n/Sn\ ,$$

for Sociotropic (N^*) effects, where the r's are sample Pearson correlations, and Se_p, Se_n, Sp and Sn are the cross-sectional sample standard deviations of e_p, e_n, P and N.[2]

Equations (21.1) and (21.2) show that the Nannestad and Paldam estimates for Egocentric and Sociotropic effects are in each case attenuated by the relative importance of errors in measurement of the politically relevant components of the Personal and National variables. The magnitudes of these biases is of course a matter of conjecture, but there is no reason at all to assume they are equal.

In the limiting case, featured in Kramer (1983), the politically relevant

---

1. Note that from the start of this chapter I implicitly have made another subtle assumption, namely that in the "true" structure of equations (12), (13) and (15.2), N and P are (in the cross-section) also uncorrelated, just as in the Nannestad and Paldam factor score set-up, so that P_i and N_i in (18) and (19) are identical. This assumption is consistent with some micro US and British set-ups used in early studies data (Kiewet, 1983, Table 6.3; Kinder and Kiewet, 1981, p. 139 and Alt, 1978 report correlations of less than 0.1 between "raw" P and N measures), but not in later ones (Kinder et al. 1989 undertook a Joreskog - confirmatory factor analysis on US data and the Personal and National factor scores they generated correlate at 0.6). The results to follow will in any case identify the main sources of bias and inconsistency in the Nannestad and Paldam estimates, but a more comprehensive picture would require that one make possible distinctions between their orthogonal Factor Scores and true P and N.

2. Alternatively, the estimates could be expressed
   $E(\hat{c}_1) = \beta_1\ bP^*,P.N + \beta_2\ bN^*,P.N = \beta_1\ r(P^*,P) \cdot SP^*/SP$,
   $E(\hat{c}_2) = \beta_1\ bP^*,N.P + \beta_2\ bN^*,N.P = \beta_2\ r(N^*,N) \cdot SN^*/SN$.

component of National economic conditions was by assumption confined to the *macro*economic effects of government policy, which are by definition fixed at any given time. Hence, the expected value (over i) of N^*_i is constant, all measured variation in voters' assessments of government responsibility for national economic conditions, N_i, must be measurement noise, and so $r(e_n, N)_i = (Se_n/Sn)_i = 1.0$. Under this view, estimates of sociotropic effects from cross-sectional set-ups like Nannestad and Paldam's are not just attenuated, but instead biased right to zero, as equation (21.2) shows.

As Kinder et al. (1989) have argued, however, voters may well differ in their evaluations of the political relevance of National economic conditions at any given time, and so cross-sectional variation in N cannot be assumed a-priori to reflect only measurement error. I regard this view as more sensible[3] and have adopted it throughout this monograph. My derivations consequently allow "true" cross-sectional variation in Sociotropic assessments.

Nonetheless, in a strong welfare state such as Denmark where the government has large distributional responsibilities, and at the same time weak (demand-side) macroeconomic capacities, one would expect

$$(22) \qquad r(e_p, P) < r(e_n, N) \text{ and } Se_p/Sp < Se_n/Sn ,$$

because at any given time government distributional policies are likely to make a stronger contribution to politically relevant cross-sectional variation of personal economic experiences than government macroeconomic policies make to politically relevant cross-sectional variation in perceptions of National economic conditions.

By comparison, although the distributional role of government is just as large in the Swedish and Norwegian welfare states as in Denmark, macroeconomic capacities are greater because of the absence of the EC-EMS constraint that effectively neutralizes Danish demand management policy. I would conjecture that the inequalities in (22) would therefore be weaker in Sweden and Norway than Denmark. And in the United States, where the

---

3. In fact, in earlier research I devoted considerable effort to establishing the heterogeneity of the electorate's responses to macroeconomic events. See Hibbs, 1987a and 1987b.

distributional relevance of government is by Nordic standards rather small and macroeconomic capacity is comparatively large, the inequalities might even be reversed.

Under strong forms of (22), which I think may well apply to Denmark, the downward bias registered by estimated Sociotropic effects will be larger than the corresponding downward bias in Egocentric effects, leading in general to an exaggerated impression of the relative importance of Personal as compared to National motivations of electoral opinion and behavior. Perhaps it should come as no surprise, then, that Nannestad and Paldam's estimates of Sociotropic effects appear weak relative to their Egocentric effects, both within their Danish cross-sectional data and by comparison to what US cross-sectional investigations have reported.

Ultimately, however, the relative importance of Egocentric and Sociotropic motivation for political opinion and behavior must be settled by empirical work rather than by appeal to plausible conjecture, as indeed it now largely has been for the United States. I give a brief account of the recent US research in the next chapter.

IX.
Recent U.S. Research on Egocentric and Sociotropic Voting

In the wake of Kramer's devastating critique of existing attempts to distinguish Sociotropic and Egocentric behavior, American researchers turned to pooled time series of cross-sections as natural data bases upon which to build proper statistical designs. The leading papers here are Marcus (1988) and (1992) and, especially, Rivers (1987). If history is any guide, these efforts will eventually set the standard elsewhere.

Pooled designs not only answer questions about the relative importance of Egocentric and Sociotropic motivation in accounting for variation in opinions and behavior across voters at any given time (the fixed time dispersion of political motivations), but also can identify the economic sources of changes through time in aggregate vote shares going to government and opposition parties. The first issue, which has been the main focus of this paper, is largely an intellectual one of interest to social scientists; the second one is what practicing politicians really care about.

To put the more recent US work in historical perspective, consider some cross-section-based estimates of Sociotropic and Egocentric influences on American Presidential voting behavior, reported in the top panel of Table 12, which are typical of the results of the first wave of US research.

The parenthesized entries in the top panel of the Table are extracted from Kinder and Kiewet's original article on American Presidential Voting behavior in 1972 and 1976. In their cross-section regressions, Sociotropic influences were found to be five to eight times bigger than Egocentric ones.[1] These were the results, replicated a number of times elsewhere, that so startled students of voting behavior and, for a time, altered the way

---

1. In fact, the multiple would have been even bigger had I added Kinder and Kiewet's "Party Competence" coefficients to the Sociotropic effects shown. As I noted in my discussion of Nannestad and Paldam's research on Competency assessments, this variable exhibited by far the greatest statistical effects in the first wave of US research on Sociotropic voting.

Table 12

The Evolution of Egocentric and Sociotropic Effects in U.S. Research
(Micro data, dependent variable is presidential vote for the candidate of the incumbent party)

OLS Cross-Section Estimates, One Election At A Time

Presidential Election	Personal Financial Situation	National Financial Average
1972	0.035	NA
	(0.070)	(0.330)
1976	0.030	NS
	(0.050)	(0.370)
1980	0.031	NA
1984	0.068	NA

Estimates From Pooled Time Series of Cross-Sections
(Purged of Politically Irrelevant Measurement Error and Estimated by Two-Stage Conditional Maximum Likelihood)

Presidential Elections	Personal	National
1956-1984 (personal Only)	0.322	NA
1956-1984 (Personal and National)	*0.288*	*0.212*

Sources: Parenthesized entries, Kinder and Kiewet (1981) table 4; all others from Rivers (1987), table 5.

---

academic political science thought about the meaning of well established connections between aggregate economic conditions and aggregate election outcomes.

The remaining entries in Table 12 are from Rivers (1987). To illustrate the scale of Egocentric effects in the conventional, cross-section tradition, Rivers computed a cross-sectional regression for each postwar presidential election of Voting support for the incumbent party's Presidential candidate on the standard Personal/Family "financial situation over the last year" question (coded +1 "better," 0 "same," and −1 "worse"), with controls for partisanship, race and union membership.

These regressions generated the usual American cross-section result of small Personal effects, quite consistent in magnitude with Kinder and Kiewet's original estimates. (In regressions for every election 1956 to 1984, the Personal Finances coefficients varied between 0.012 and 0.068, with a mean 0.034. I have excerpted only the 1972 to 1984 estimates here.) Such small micro level Personal effects are able to account for only a tiny fraction of the established time series response of aggregate voting outcomes to aggregate income changes.

In aggregate time series studies for the United States, real income growth has repeatedly proven to be the best economic predictor of election outcomes. (Erikson, 1989 reviews the models.) Hence, not surprisingly, both Rivers and Marcus, who developed pooled time series of cross-sections designs at about the same time, used income variables to test for Egocentric and Sociotropic motivations. They specify models of the form

$$(23) \qquad V_{it} = \beta_1 \, P_{it} + \beta_2 \, N_t + Z_{it}'\gamma,$$

where P_{it} represents micro data on the Personal/Family Finances question, N is a National average income variable (which therefore varies over t but not i) and Z is a matrix of control variables, including partisanship.[2] Hence, the effects of Egocentric motivation are estimated by β_1 — individuals' voting responses to changes in their *own* income — and Sociotropic effects are estimated by β_2 — individuals' voting responses to changes in *national* average income.

---

2. In set-ups like this, as Fiorina (1977) first emphasized and has been reinforced by MacKuen et al.'s subsequent work (1989), partisanship can be taken to represent the effects of distributed (retrospective) lags of the other variables, by essentially the same reasoning that led to the appearance of lagged V_{it} in the dynamic solutions (5a)-5(b). This implies that the estimates obtained should be interpreted as "impact multipliers" (contemporaneous effects) that may yield the correct relative magnitudes but not the correct total magnitudes of Egocentric and Sociotropic effects.

Pooling alone is no panacea, however, as here too measurement error problems arise, although they are likely to be less severe than in pure cross-section studies. In Marcus' model average national income, N, is measured by national accounts data on per capita real personal disposable income growth, which he assumes measures politically relevant National economic performance without error. Marcus takes a brute force econometric approach to measurement errors in P_{it}, and just applies Instrumental Variables using, what looks to me to be, a fairly arbitrary list of instruments.[3] Nonetheless, Marcus' pooled Instrumental Variables estimates of Egocentric effects run about three times bigger than those reported in OLS cross-sections.

Rivers' approach is a good deal more ingenious. Building on the framework initially laid out by Kramer (1983), Rivers' set-up has greater internal consistency than Marcus' in the sense that N_t is the mean over i at each t of P_{it}; $N_{it} = E(P_{it}|t)$. More important, this allows Rivers to exploit higher moments of the income distribution (which is nonstationary because the mean and variance of P_{it} shifts through time) to identify the politically relevant fraction of income changes.[4]

Rivers, 'Two-Stage Conditional Maximum Likelihood' (2SCML) regressions, abstracted in the lower panel of Table 12, produce coefficients that are purged of politically irrelevant measurement errors, which are estimated to comprise about 50% of the total variance in the Family Finances question. The contrast to the OLS estimates is dramatic. Considered alone, the effect of Personal income change on Presidential Voting choices under 2SCML estimation is around seven times bigger than the average OLS estimate. And considered jointly with National income changes, Personal effects are around 35 percent larger than National effects (0.288 versus 0.212). By comparison, the heavily biased estimates populating the initial research of Kinder and Kiewet and others implied that

---

3. Marcus' instruments evidently include other variables from the survey pertaining to income and spending.
4. The basic strategy amounts to comparing shifts in the mean and variance of P_{it} to shifts in voting outcomes. The electoral consequences of shifts in the variance of P_{it} conveys information about the fraction of income change that is politically relevant.

National effects were eight times or more bigger than Personal effects.[5]

The best estimates currently available for US Presidential Voting behavior indicate, then, that both Egocentric and Sociotropic motivation are important, with the former exerting somewhat greater influence than the later. This is quite a far cry from the more or less total dominance of Sociotropic motivation claimed in the first wave of research on the United States and some other countries. Indeed, had we known in 1979-80 what Rivers via Kramer has taught us in the years since, it is doubtful that there ever would have been much of a Sociotropic school of voting behavior in the first place.

---

5. Rivers finds National effects to be as much as twelve times bigger Personal effects in Pooled OLS regressions, which strongly illustrates the point that pooling by itself is no solution to the measurement bias problem.

X.
Summary and Conclusions

A strong tenet of traditional economic theory is that individual economic behavior is governed more or less wholly by attempts to maximize self-interest. Applied to connections between economic conditions and political opinion and behavior, the self-interest presumption became known as "pocketbook" voting. Voters rewarded parties that advanced their own economic interests and punished those that threatened them.

The pocketbook view, or "egocentric" view as I frequently have referred to it in this monograph, was the prevailing interpretation of relations between economics and politics until Kinder and Kiewet's work appeared in the late 1970s and early 1980s. Evaluating the pocketbook hypothesis with micro, survey data on US voting behavior, Kinder and Kiewet found that personal economic experiences seemed to exert much weaker influence on electoral behavior than voters' evaluations of national economic conditions and their assessments of the government's performance and competence in dealing with national problems. They labeled the phenomenon sociotropic voting: "... sociotropic citizens vote according to the country's pocketbook, not their own."

Replications Kinder and Kiewet's research were at first done mainly by other American researchers, and on the whole the results were supportive of the sociotropic thesis. Michael Lewis-Beck's (1988) comparative investigation of five European countries, based on the 1983 and 1984 Eurobarometer Surveys, was the most ambitious study, and he too concluded that sociotropic variables had considerably greater impact on European parliamentary voting behavior than egocentric variables. Yet Lewis-Beck also found that questions that explicitly prompted survey respondents to assess the effect of *Government* on national or personal economic conditions tended to show stronger effects than the same assessments made without the Government responsibility filter. This is precisely the result that Kramer's (1983) analysis would have anticipated.

Systematic evaluation of the importance of sociotropic and egocentric motivation of political attitudes and behavior came somewhat later to

Denmark than elsewhere, notably with the early 1990's research of Jørgen Goul Andersen, Søren Winter and Poul Erik Mouritzen, and Peter Nannestad and Martin Paldam. Nannestad and Paldam's work was geared more explicitly to the international debate and made use of higher powered statistical methods than the other studies, and for these reasons was taken as the point of reference for much of this monograph.

Moreover, whereas Goul Andersen came pretty squarely down on the side of a sociotropic Danish voter, and Winter and Mouritzen painted a mixed picture of a citizenry governed by both individualist and collectivist motives, Nannestad and Paldam's Danish voter was driven almost exclusively by egocentric concerns. Nannestad and Paldam's conclusions, therefore, departed substantially from those of the other Danish investigators, as well as from those turned in by the first (mainly sociotropic) and second (mixed sociotropic-egocentric) waves of US research.

However, as I argued in chapters 2 and 3, Nannestad and Paldam's empirical work in fact yielded little or no evidence favoring an egocentric model of Danish Voting choices. To begin with, as in traditional electoral studies undertaken for Denmark and other Scandinavian countries, their data showed that Danish Bloc Voting intentions are extremely sluggish; only a tiny fraction of the electorate reported crossing Party Bloc lines from one election to the other. And the small fraction of Bloc switchers that was observed in their surveys evidently was motivated mainly by evaluations of the governing Bloc's (implicitly relative) management Competence. In the presence of prior Bloc Vote and Competency rating of the government, other variables exerted little or no effect on Bloc Voting intentions in their regressions.

To a good first approximation, therefore, Nannestad and Paldam's work, properly interpreted, implies that Danish Bloc Voting behavior evolves very nearly as a random walk perturbed by Competency "shocks," that is, by shifts in public perceptions of the government's management ability. In ordinary language, this simply means that the long-run time path of micro Bloc Voting choices in Denmark has been driven by the cumulative (rather modestly discounted) history of each voter's assessment of the governing bloc's Competency.

Moreover, since Party Competence assessments comprised the most important indicator of sociotropic motivation in the founding work on the topic, by established standards of the field Nannestad and Paldam's research actually demonstrated that *sociotropic* orientations have dominated Bloc Voting outcomes in Denmark. Here I share the working assumption of Jørgen Goul Andersen, who, like Kinder and Kiewet and most other contributors to the field, also regarded evaluations of the Government's problem solving ability as a measure of sociotropic orientation.

The sources of shifts in the electorate's assessment of government Competency, therefore, is the place to look for specific sociotropic and egocentric effects on Danish voting outcomes, and in this respect Nannestad and Paldam's analyses of the determinants of Competency ratings took on added significance. Their first line of analysis investigated statistical relations between aggregate Competency ratings and changes of the inflation rate, changes of the growth rate of real wages, changes of the unemployment rate and changes of the balance of payments surplus/deficit from 1983 to 1991. Nannestad and Paldam interpreted the results of these macro political-economic analyses as favoring an egocentric or self-interest model of political evaluation, but as I showed in chapter 6 no such conclusion can be drawn from their aggregate time series regressions. Although of some intrinsic interest to the study of economics and politics, regressions with aggregated data of the sort undertaken by Nannestad and Paldam register, by construction, both egocentric *and* sociotropic effects.

Most of the Nannestad and Paldam's research on the determinants of variation in Competency ratings, however, was devoted to investigating sociotropic and egocentric effects at the micro level in a 1990-91 cross-section. Here again they concluded that egocentric variables dominated but, as I argued at some length in chapters 3 to 8, their analyses were severely flawed. I identified three main problems.

The first problem is simple, yet quite basic. Specific sociotropic concerns (recall that the Competency variable itself is best thought of as a general sociotropic variable) were not properly measured. The Social Worries variables (Unemployment, Inflation and Foreign Debt) which were assumed to tap sociotropic concerns, and hence were used to form a composite Sociotropic Factor Score, have exactly the same deficiency as the macroeconomic variables in Nannestad and Paldam's aggregate regressions for Competency ratings: In principle worrying about unemployment, inflation, or even the foreign debt, may reflect (and in practice almost certainly does reflect) both egocentric and sociotropic orientations. In the absence of a clear measure of sociotropic motivation, it obviously was not possible for Nannestad and Paldam or anyone else to make credible inferences about the relative importance of self-interest and national interest in accounting for voters' assessments of Government management or problem solving Competency.

Second, Nannestad and Paldam's empirical work showed that the Foreign Debt Worry constituent variable of their Sociotropic Factor Score exhibited positive effects on Voting Intentions for (and, presumably, Competency ratings of) Bourgeois Governments, whereas Unemployment and Inflation Worries exhibited negative effects. Consequently, when combined (added up after weighting) to form a common Factor Score, the effects of the worry variables tended to neutralize each other (cancel out), thereby driving the coefficient of the composite Sociotropic Factor Score toward zero.

As I emphasized in chapter 3, however, rational voters would be expected to gravitate toward a Conservative government when Foreign Debt "worries" loomed large in their minds, as long as Conservative governments were viewed as more competent on dealing with the debt issue than the Socialist opposition, as Nannestad and Paldam in fact claimed they were. Though Nannestad and Paldam's work is based quite self-consciously on the rational behavior paradigm developed in economics, their construction of a Sociotropic Factor Score violated a fundamental tenet of the theory of rational choice: Rational Voters should choose the Party perceived as delivering the better (utility maximizing) performance on issues of concern ("worries").

Third, as Kramer (1983) first pointed out, cross-section analyses, like those undertaken by Nannestad and Paldam and many others before, are inherently limited when it comes to identifying the politically relevant components of economic performance. Under a narrow interpretation of Kramer's argument, the politically relevant fraction of measured economic experience is just the government-induced macroeconomic component, which necessarily is nil in cross-sections. But Kramer's devastating critique of cross-section based research was cast in overly strict terms. As Kinder et al. (1989) argued, voters may well differ in their evaluations of the political relevance of national economic conditions at fixed points in time, and so cross-sectional variation in economic experiences and assessments cannot be regarded a-priori as being irrelevant to the calibration of sociotropic and egocentric political motivation.

Nonetheless, Kramer's fundamental argument, which I generalized a bit in chapters 4 and 5 to accommodate true cross-sectional variation in politically relevant economic experience, helps explain why the cross-sectional evidence presented in chapters 1, 7 and 8 on various political choices in different countries and times, conveyed such a mixed and unstable message concerning the relative importance of egocentric and sociotropic political motivation. Moreover, application of Kramer-inspired measurement error econometrics to the case of Denmark, where the government has large distributional responsibilities and at the same time weak demand-side macroeconomic capacities (because of the EC-EMS constraint), led me to conjecture in chapter 8 that the downward bias registered by estimated sociotropic effects was likely to have been substantially greater than the corresponding bias registered by estimated egocentric effects in Nannestad and Paldam's cross-section regressions.

All things considered, then, Nannestad and Paldam's work most likely gives a much exaggerated impression of the influence of personal-egocentric as compared to national-sociotropic motivations of Danish political opinion and behavior. Yet, in the last analysis, the relative importance of egoism and solidarity in political life can be resolved only by empirical work, not by informed conjecture or theoretical reasoning. In this connection, I reviewed in chapter 9 the evolution of research methods and results on egocentric and sociotropic voting in the United States. The U.S. record illustrates vividly how on occasion refinement of research design and statistical methodology can actually change the *qualitative* implications of the evidence.

In the first wave of cross-section based research on the United States, sociotropic effects were estimated to be from eight to twelve times larger than egocentric effects. Relative magnitudes of this order were what gave rise to the Sociotropic school of voting, launched by Kinder and Kiewet's germinal research. In the aftermath of Kramer's critique, however, American researchers turned to time series of cross-sections data bases, and applied alternatives to Ordinary Least Squares, to obtain estimates purged of errors in measurement. As a result of this second round of research, egocentric motivation of American voting behavior, once believed to be of only minor importance, is now believed to exert roughly the same, or perhaps somewhat greater, influence as sociotropic motivation.

I think it likely that once sociotropic orientations are better measured for Denmark, application of appropriate estimators and pooled time series of cross-sections statistical designs will occasion analogous revisions of Nannestad and Paldam's current estimates of the relative importance of egocentric and sociotropic motivation. For the reasons developed earlier, however, I would expect the second wave of Danish research to yield an enlargement of Sociotropic effects, now claimed by Nannestad and Paldam to exert such feeble influence on Danish political opinion and behavior.

Finally, let me step back for a moment from all the factor analyses, regressions, measurement error biases and the like populating this monograph, and remark on the larger forces that have shaped the evolution of the Danish political economy. As an outside, American observer it seems obvious that in Denmark, as well as in the other advanced welfare states of the West, solidarity or sociotropic motivation must have exercised quite decisive influence on long-run political behavior, policy formation and institutional design.

After all the advanced welfare state represents a social experiment of enormous proportions that socialized the consumption and distribution of six-teenths or more of national income and succeeded in offsetting most of the least attractive consequences of unfettered market capitalism. All but truly residual poverty has been eliminated and a generous security floor below which no, or at least very few, citizens are permitted to fall was erected. Despite all the distortions and disincentives created, and the "waste, fraud and abuse" (to borrow from Ronald Reagan's characterization of America's rather modest public budget) that are bound to accompany a public service and income security system of the scale of Denmark's, it is difficult not to interpret the Danish welfare state as quite dramatic evidence of the politics of solidarity.

SOLIDARITY OR EGOISM

References

Aardal, Bengt and Ola Listhaug, 1986, "Economic Factors and Voting Behavior in Norway 1965-1985," Trondheim, Institute for Social Research.

Alt, James, 1978, *The Politics of Economic Decline*, Cambridge University Press.

Amemiya, Takeshi, 1981., "Qualitative Response Models: A Survey," *Journal of Economic Literature*, 4, 1483-1536.

Amemiya, Takeshi, 1985, *Advanced Econometrics*, Harvard University Press.

Chappel, Henry and William Keech, 1985, "A New View of Political Accountability for Economic Performance," *American Political Science Review*, 79, 10-27.

Downs, Anthony, 1957, *An Economic Theory of Democracy*, New York: Harper and Row.

Erikson, Robert, 1989, "Economic Conditions and the Presidential Vote," *American Political Science Review*, 83, 567-576.

Fair, Ray, 1978, "The Effect of Economic Events on Votes for President," *The Review of Economics and Statistics*, 60, 169-173.

Fiorina, Morris, 1977, "An Outline of a Model of Party Choice," *American Journal of Political Science,* 13, 601-625.

Fiorina, Morris, 1978, "Economic Retrospective Voting in American National Elections: A Micro-Analysis," *American Journal of Political Science*, 23, 426-443.

Fiorina, Morris, 1981, *Retrospective Voting in American National Elections*, Yale University Press.

Gilljam, Mikael and Holmberg, Sören Holmberg, 1992, *Väljarna inför 90-Talet*, Gothenburg University, Mimeo.

Goul Andersen, Jørgen, 1992a, "Årsager Til Mistillid" in Andersen et al. *Vi og Vore Politikere*, Copenhagen: Spektrum.

Goul Andersen, Jørgen, 1992b, *Politisk Mistillid i Danmark*, Institut for Statskundskab, Aarhus Universitet.

Goul Andersen, Jørgen, 1992c, "Politikerleden, Myte eller Realitet" in Andersen et al. *Vi og Vore Politikere*, Copenhagen: Spektrum.

Granberg, Donald and Holmberg, Sören, 1986, "Political Perception Among Voters in Sweden and the U.S." *Western Political Quarterly*, March 7-28.

Holmberg, Sören, 1984, *Väljare i Förändring*, Stockholm: Libro.

Holmberg, Sören and Gilljam, Mikael, 1986, *Väljare och Val i Sverige*, Stockholm: Bonniers.

Hibbs, Douglas, 1987a, *The American Political Economy: Macroeconomic and Electoral Politics*, Harvard University Press.

Hibbs, Douglas, 1987b, *The Political Economy of Industrial Democracies*, Harvard University Press.

Key, V.O., 1966, *The Responsible Electorate*, New York: Vintage.

Kiewiet, D. Roderick, 1983, *Macroeconomics and Micropolitics*, University of Chicago Press.

Kiewiet, D. Roderick, 1981, "Policy Oriented Voting in Response to Economic Issues," *American Journal of Political Science*, 75, 448-459.

Kiewiet, D. Roderick and Douglas Rivers, 1985, " A Retrospective on Retrospective Voting," in Heinz Eulau and Michael Lewis-Beck, eds., *Economic Conditions and Electoral Outcomes*, New York: Agathon.

Kinder, Donald and D. Roderick Kiewet, 1979, "Economic Discontent and Political Behavior: The Role of Personal Grievances and Collective Economic Judgements in Congressional Voting," *American Journal of Political Science*, 23, 495-527.

Kinder, Donald and D. Roderick Kiewet, 1981, "Sociotropic Politics: The American Case," *British Journal of Political Science*, 11, 129-161.

Kinder, Donald, et al.,1989, "Economics and Politics in the 1984 American Presidential Election," *American Journal of Political Science,* 33, 491-515.

Kramer, Gerald, 1971, "Short Term Fluctuations in US Voting Behavior, 1896-1964," *American Political Science Review*, 65, 131-143.

Kramer, Gerald, 1983, "The Ecological Fallacy Revisited: Aggregate-Versus Individual-Level Findings on Economics and Elections, and Sociotropic Voting," *American Political Science Review*, 77, 92-111.

Lewin, Leif, 1991, *Self-Interest and Public Interest in Western Politics*, Oxford University Press.

Lewis-Beck, Michael, 1988, *Economics and Elections: The Major Western Democracies*, Ann Arbor: University of Michigan Press

Listhaug, Ola, 1989a, *Citizens, Parties and Norwegian Electoral Politics 1957-1985*, Oslo: Tapir.

Listhaug, Ola, 1989b, "Økonomie og Stemmigiving" in Vernt Aardal and Henry Valen, eds. *Velgere, Partier og Politisk Avstand*, Oslo, Statistisk Centralbyro.

MacKuen, Michael, et al., 1989, "Macropartisanship," *American Political Science Review*, 83, 1125-1142.

Maddala, G.S., 1983, *Limited-Dependent and Qualitative Variables in Econometrics*, Cambridge University Press.

Marcus, Gregory, 1988, "The Impact of Personal and National Economic Conditions on the Presidential Vote: A Pooled Cross-section Analysis," *American Journal of Political Science*, 32, 137-154.

Marcus, Gregory, 1992, "The Impact of Personal and National Economic Conditions on Presidential Voting, 1956-1988," *American Journal of Political Science*, 36, 829-834.

Meehl, Paul, 1977, "The Selfish Voter Paradox and the Thrown-Away Vote Argument," *American Political Science Review*, 71, 11-30.

Miller, Arthur and Ola Listhaug, 1984, "Economic Effects on the Vote in Norway," *Political Behavior*, 4, 301-19.

Mouritzen, Poul, 1987, "The Demanding Citizen: Driven by Policy, Self-Interest or Ideology?" *European Journal of Political Research*, 15, 417-435.

Nannestad, Peter and Martin Paldam, 1991, "Between Good Citizenship and Self-Interest: Economics, Private Economy and Distrust of the Government's Competence," August, Aarhus University, Mimeo.

Nannestad, Peter and Martin Paldam, 1992, Economic Grievances and Government Support in a Small Welfare State: Micro Theory and the Danish Case," 27 August, Aarhus University Working Paper.

Nannestad, Peter and Martin Paldam, 1993a, "Sammenhængen mellem samfundsøkonomi, privatøkonomi og tilslutningen til regeringspartierne," 2. iteration, Aarhus University, Mimeo, in progress.

Nannestad, Peter and Martin Paldam, 1993b, "The VP Function: A Survey of the Literature on Vote and Popularity Functions after 25 Years," forthcoming *Public Choice*.

Nielsen, Hans Jørgen, 1992, "A Basic Question and an Utopian Goal," in Peter Gundelach and Karen Siune, eds. *From Voters to Participants*, Aarhus: Politica.

Paldam, Martin, 1981, "A Preliminary Survey of Theories and Findings on Vote and Popularity Functions," *European Journal of Political Research*, 9, 181-199.

Peltzman, Sam, 1990, "How Efficient Is The Vote Market," *Journal of Law and Economics*, April, 27-63.

Rivers, Douglas, 1987, "Microeconomics and Macroeconomics: A Solution to the Kramer Problem," California Institute of Technology, forthcoming, *American Political Science Review*.

Tonsgaard, Ole, 1989, "Vælgervandringer og Vælgerusikkerhed," chapter 5 in J. Elklit and O. Tonsgaard, eds. *To Folketingsvalg*, Aarhus: Politica.

Winter, Søren and Poul Erik Mouritzen, "Are Voters Naive Egoists?" Institut for Statskundskab, Aarhus University, 1992.

Publications from the Rockwool Foundation Research Unit

Time and Consumption
edited by Gunnar Viby Mogensen
Central Bureau of Statistics (Danmarks Statistik), 1990

Unemployment and Flexibility on the Danish Labour Market
by Gunnar Viby Mogensen
Central Bureau of Statistics (Danmarks Statistik), 1993

Solidarity or Egoism?
The Economics of Sociotropic and Egocentric Influences on Political
Behaviour: Denmark in International and Theoretical Perspective
by Douglas A. Hibbs
Aarhus University Press, 1993

Danes and Their Politicians
by Gunnar Viby Mogensen
Aarhus University Press, 1993

Welfare and Work Incentives. A North European Perspective
edited by A.B. Atkinson and Gunnar Viby Mogensen
Oxford University Press, 1993

Index

SOLIDARITY OR EGOISM